That *HEARING*

They Shall *PERCEIVE*

That
HEARING
They Shall
PERCEIVE

Charles Duell Kean

 NEW YORK • 1963

ACKNOWLEDGMENTS

Grateful acknowledgment is made for permission to use the following copyrighted material:

Karl Barth, quotation from his sermon "Repentance" in *Come Holy Spirit.*

The Church Hymnal Corporation, Hymns 354 and 494, in *The Hymnal, 1940.*

The Church Society for College Work, quotation from *The Church Review,* May, 1940.

Walter Lippmann, quotation from his syndicated column in *The Washington Post.*

PREFACE

WHEN I was invited to give the headline series of daily lectures at the Sewanee Summer Conference for 1960, it was suggested that what the committee was looking for was a presentation, in modern terms, of the great traditional verities of the Christian Faith. The more I thought about this request, however, the more my mind kept returning to the problem: it is not so much a question of stating and restating the verities, even in modern terms, as it is of modern man being able to hear them when they are proclaimed. This became the burden of the lecture series.

A year later I was asked to accept a similar responsibility at the Hood College Conference, the adult conference for the Episcopal Church in the Middle Atlantic States, in 1961. I was again challenged by the problem which I had tried to deal with the previous year—that man in modern culture

5

finds it very difficult to hear, in terms addressed to his own situation, what the Christian Faith is really saying. In February, 1962, I undertook the same task in a series of lectures to a conference of Episcopal clergymen at the College of Preachers, Washington Cathedral.

This book is the result, not only of three series of lectures on the same subject, but also of reaction from and discussion with some of those who heard these thoughts presented. I am particularly indebted to the Rev. David B. Collins, Chaplain of the University of the South, who also served as Chaplain of the Sewanee Conference, and enabled me to have tape recordings of the first series. I am also indebted to the Rev. John O'Hear, Rector of Christ Church, Christiana Hundred, Delaware, who served as Chaplain of the Hood College Conference, and to the Rev. Frederick H. Arterton, Warden of the College of Preachers.

Besides the inspiration given me by the above, I also wish to thank Mrs. Ellason Downs of Greenville, Delaware; the Rev. Herschel G. Miller, Chaplain of Norwich University, Northfield, Vermont; Dr. Kenneth A. Bohr, of the staff of the World Bank; and my brother, John V. Kean of Providence, R. I., for reading the manuscript with an eye to its usefulness for thoughtful lay people.

CHARLES D. KEAN

CONTENTS

CONTENTS

That *HEARING*

They Shall *PERCEIVE*

1

CHRISTIAN FAITH AND MODERN CULTURE

THE CHRISTIAN FAITH claims that its message is directed to every man, woman, and child in every country under the sun, in every social condition, in every changing circumstance that can possibly develop. This claim to universality is as much a part of the Gospel as the proclamation that God has acted in history through the saving life, death and resurrection of Jesus Christ. Through making the claim that God's action is relevant to every possible human situation, the Christian faith denies that it is only one of many optional ways of looking at life, but rather insists it is the only approach which makes possible an appreciation in depth of life's fundamental meaning and purpose.

Once the claim has been made, however, it must be admitted that there is a continual problem of re-translation, not simply re-phrasing the language in a modern idiom, but

11

rather re-thinking the issue—the meaning of man's confusion in God's scheme of things—so that living men and women may see that the Christian message touches them where they are. This task of re-translation must be undertaken by each succeeding generation and, in a sense, by every individual man and woman if the connection between the Gospel and the human situation is to become clear.

In twentieth-century culture, the connection between the Christian faith and the predicament in which man finds himself—at home, in business, in the community, and in the larger world—is neither obvious nor direct. If, indeed, every age has the same task of re-translation, in ours the problem has acquired new dimensions that at one and the same time make it more urgent and more difficult. The emerging age of space and speed made possible by modern science, on the one hand, and the development of unprecedented power as a means of attaining political goals, on the other hand, raise questions as to man's destiny in a way the world has never known before.

It is important to recognize at the outset, however, that not only is the Christian faith faced with a more difficult task in translating its message so that it can be heard by modern man, but even more the culture in which men and women hear any message has itself become confused. There are serious questions as to how far its categories of interpretation enable those who live within it, and who cannot possibly step outside it, to deal adequately with their individual and social experience.

By culture, I mean the variegated fabric of traditions, values and understandings that people take for granted, and which give function and purpose to the political, economic, and social institutions that frame their lives. Our culture

12

gives us the tools with which we think. Indeed, we cannot even dream except by the use of categories which we inherited rather than invented. Dr. Clifford L. Stanley, of the Virginia Theological Seminary, used to say that Robinson Crusoe on his desert island had to think like a seventeenth-century Englishman because he knew nothing different and could explain his predicament in no other way. And when Friday came along, there was the British colonial system of that day!

When President John F. Kennedy reported by television to the American people after his meeting with Premier Khrushchev in Vienna in May, 1961, he pointed out that when westerners use such phrases as "good" and "evil," "democracy" and "liberty," in conversation with those from the other side of the iron curtain, these very words instead of helping to clarify the subject under discussion add to the confusion, because they are taken to mean something different on one side of the ideological barrier than on the other. While the President did not say so in so many words, the problem is not simply one of dictionary definitions nor even of semantics, but rather one of what really makes life worth living for individuals and provides significant goals for society.

In other words, the present polarization of power between two world centers and the struggle for the minds of, as well as the political influence over, the uncommitted peoples of the earth points up the fact that western culture, as we have known it, cannot assume it has universal relevance. Since the Christian faith can only speak to western men and women through the instrumentalities of their culture, is it by this fact limited only to those who think in western terms? Furthermore, is it doomed by the present inadequacies of western culture to be ineffective elsewhere as a faith to live by?

Not only is this question raised sharply by the way the Communist bloc countries have developed a culture, different in many respects if not in every particular, from our ways of interpreting things, it is also raised by developments in the so-called younger nations. I am indebted to Bishop Michael Hollis, formerly of Madras, for the following illustration. In a Ramakrishna temple outside Calcutta there are statues of the great religious figures of world history—the Guatama Buddha, Confucius, Moses, Jesus, and Mohammed. The peculiar thing is that the figure of Jesus is carrying a spoon. When the visitor asks why, the guide explains, "Jesus is a westerner. He cannot eat without a spoon." In other words, Christianity is regarded by many people in other parts of the world as being only the religious face of western culture, more often specifically Anglo-American culture. This fact is also borne out by the inroads Islamic missionaries are currently making among the Christian Negroes of Africa at the very moment they are thinking of national self-determination.

Some Notes of Western Culture

There are many things that can be said about western culture, as we have inherited it and as it provides the framework for our thinking. Four points are perhaps sufficient to show how it partly confuses the problem which confronts modern man and why the Christian faith cannot allow itself simply to be identified with that culture as its religious face.

1. Regardless of what we say in words, the prevailing pattern of the western world assumes that a man is worth what he owns, what he can earn, or what he can produce. This presupposition has become dominant since the Renaissance and has largely been taken for granted during the past three

hundred years. The term "the pocketbook nerve" is one illustration of the point. Such other terms as "the profit motive" and "economic determinism" tend to indicate that acquisitiveness is understood to be the key to both individual behavior and social change. "Free enterprise" suggests that the most important component of freedom is the ability to make money, and "enlightened self-interest," instead of suggesting a moral limitation on acquisitiveness, points out the desirability of modifying one's immediate grasp in the interest of longer-term results.

These comments on what are taken for granted in so much of the western world are not made as an indictment. The theory that economic value is primary has had much to do with the building of modern civilization. While moral and spiritual questions have been raised all along from within this culture that assumed the primacy of economic value, the immediate problem is somewhere else. Does this tradition really deal adequately with human motivations, individual and social? Are not men and women actually willing to forego economic advantage because other concerns have greater appeal? It is only since the middle 1930's, however, that there has been any general appreciation of the fact that political power has a dynamic of its own quite distinct from economics.

2. The economic understanding of social value has always allowed for political power as a real factor in the social process, but only within the last two generations has there been any widespread appreciation of the fact that power is often prior to, rather than a means for, economic advantage. When someone reminded Stalin of the tremendous influence of the Pope in southern Europe and throughout the world, the Russian dictator is said to have remarked, "How many

15

divisions does he have?" This cynical appraisal of political reality is not something peculiar to the other side of the iron curtain, even though there may be distinct understandings there as to the components of political power. The vicissitudes that have beset American foreign policy since the end of World War II may indeed be partly due to a failure to appreciate the independence of political power from economic considerations, but perhaps they are more seriously due to a loss of the American power position for a variety of tactical reasons so that when bargaining was called for, the counters at our disposal were limited in value.

3. Our culture has a most ambivalent view of personality. It sets very high store on individuality and at the same time depreciates the social value of personhood. The result is that there is a very real split between freedom and responsibility. This makes it difficult for many Americans to understand why some of the peoples in the underdeveloped nations of the world do not set as high a premium on the franchise as we think they ought to when the problem of land ownership is unresolved. Within the culture itself, freedom tends to be thought of as disengagement, freedom from obligation and involvement, while responsibility tends to be understood as a limitation upon liberty. In the huge concentrations of population that mark most major American cities, the point is illustrated by the mass provisions for both housing and employment, where people resemble interchangeable nuts and bolts in a bin, yet where every man and woman thinks of himself as having an impregnable private life.

4. Our culture is strongly influenced by what is best called scientism, which is an attitude toward science to which many scientists do not themselves subscribe yet which has been pervasive for several decades in educational circles and very

16

influential in the forming of public policy. By oversimplification, scientism can be summarized by saying that only that which can be measured is real, with the implication that if value is to have substance, it must be determined in this manner. There is the further implication that that which cannot be measured is unreal.

Scientism is obviously an extension to the whole picture of man's life and work of that which is quite proper in the physical sciences. A method that has solid results in the fields of chemistry and physics, for example, can have considerable usefulness when applied to the social sciences—such as economics and sociology and political science—provided the student realizes that he is dealing with abstractions from reality rather than the actualities themselves. The usefulness continues, but the danger is heightened when one studies personality and subjects people to the procedures of the laboratory. In any event, the experience of the past half-century demonstrates that whenever generalizations from the physical sciences are made the key to social and historical interpretation, the dynamic factors instead of being explained will be filtered out. When this happens, people are unable to appreciate the real nature of their problems.

This cultural pattern did not develop overnight. It has evolved for centuries. While it can be easily analyzed in a derogatory manner by those who like to tilt at windmills, the very persistence of our social institutions—adapting themselves to changing political and economic situations down to the present day—indicates that there is a vitality in the culture. Perhaps this vitality may be running out, yet it is far from spent at the present time. Nevertheless, the nature of the political and economic crises of our age suggests: (a) that the western world does not have cultural resources sufficiently

17

elastic either to appreciate or to deal with the agenda before it, and (b) that the very maintenance of these cultural patterns in an age when they appear to be obsolescent makes it difficult for modern man to hear what the Christian faith has to say.

Faith and Culture

The Christian faith has to be proclaimed to people so that they can hear what it has to say about the meaning of their lives and the situations within which they find themselves. It will not be classical Christianity if it appears to take men and women out of history, as if what is happening in Europe, Asia and Africa, as well as within the United States, did not matter. It will not be the faith of the Cross and the Resurrection if it seeks to minimize the fear and anxiety which continue to haunt the lives of individuals and to confuse the social process. If it is true, the faith must be proclaimed in such a way that those whose lives are conditioned by modern western culture may hear its message but not in such a way that it appears to be limited to them alone.

People make their faith their own in the course of dealing with the practical decisions of everyday affairs on every level, and these affairs are framed by the political, economic and social structures in which they occur. A dynamic faith, therefore, is one which enables those who hold it to accept the real pressures of the times without either faking or running away, but rather gives its holders a creative imagination with which to see through the present confusion to the ultimate purpose of the glory of God. This is the agelong message of the Gospel of Jesus Christ, speaking just as surely to twentieth-century man in this world of space and speed and changing landmarks as to any other.

There is a spiritual dimension to the problem of man living with himself and his neighbor as he faces his historic destiny. Yet this spiritual dimension is not being adequately realized in our day because the culture and the faith are not speaking effectively to each other. Cultures of their own logic tend to arrogate the role of faith to themselves, and western culture is no exception. To the extent that this prevails, men and women are encouraged to find meaning for their lives by identifying themselves with what is—the American way of life or the inalienable right of self-determination by individuals, minorities, or even majorities. Then that which is overtly religious is valuable only insofar as it supports the cultural claim. The perennial role of prophetic religion, however, is to undercut continually the pretensions of the status quo, whatever it is, to be self-sufficient. This has been done over and over again in the long Judaeo-Christian tradition by raising such graphic symbols as "The Day of the Lord" or "The City of God," which suggest that the world's ways are subject to judgment by some higher standard than the world's desires.

In eras of relative political and economic stability the tension between the faith and culture is often unnoticed, but in an age like ours, when the culture itself is threatened with a loss of self-confidence, there is a crying need for the prophetic role of faith. When Alaric the Visigoth sacked Rome in the year 410, St. Augustine pointed the imagination of his generation beyond the City of this World to the City of God, not as if the fall of Rome did not matter, because it did, because it meant the end of an era of security, but because imaginative social reconstruction could not take place without a new perspective. We live in an age not unlike St. Augustine's, regardless of how the fate of the two Berlins and the two Germanys is ultimately settled, regardless of how the struggle for the control of Southeast Asia materializes, regardless of the outcome of the social upheaval in Latin America.

Has western culture lost its nerve? There are indications that this has happened. To the extent it has, it needs not peace talks but judgment. To the extent that modern men and women can face what is implied by this, there is hope for reconciliation and a peace which passeth all understanding. But this is only possible on the basis of a dynamic faith which takes seriously the actualities with which men and women are confronted. It can never take place so long as the Christian Gospel is understood to be an official set of opinions about God, man and the universe to which one ought to subscribe, but which can only be connected with daily affairs by ethical imperatives.

Faith, in the last analysis, is always the commitment of one's self on the basis of a conviction that here is life and reality and, therefore, here and here only must one stand and act. The best analogue for faith is that of marriage, particularly where it occurs after a period of courtship and with some serious premarital counseling. When young people enter marriage in this context, they will have had conferences with physicians and clergymen, read books, considered the various aspects of the in-law situation, and made tentative economic plans. The whole process will have taken considerable time and effort, and one thing is certain: they are not acting blindly. But if they wait until the last possible bit of information is procured, they will wait until one of the two is carried out in a box. If there is to be any marriage at all, therefore,

20

he couple has to leap beyond the limit of human understand-
ng *as if* their meeting were made in heaven.

Christian faith takes seriously the historic situation in
which people find themselves. It takes seriously our individual and social failures of omission and commission. It is
willing to look frankly at the fact of physical death for men
and women and ultimate decline for social institutions. Then,
while facing the facts of life as honestly as possible, it affirms
the fact that leaps beyond human understanding—that my
own personal value, and hence that of other people too, is
determined by the life, death and resurrection of the Son of
God. Therefore, God has placed his stamp of value on my
life in a way that I can never do for myself. Christian faith
is the conviction that in accepting Jesus Christ as my Savior,
I discover that I live in a new and transformed relationship
both to the Most High God and to the family of the children
of God.

Christian faith is not abstract opinion. Its cutting edge is
in the fact that I know myself to be forgiven and that, therefore, I can live with the actuality of failure here and now.
Although guilt and anxiety will continue to arise, I can look
beyond them to a love which loved me since before the world
began. Although fear will always in one way or another dog
my footsteps, I am also aware of the love that casts out fear.
In spite of the fact that death remains the great unavoidable
question mark, I am supported by a presence that goes with
me through the shadow. This means that I can let other
people love me and I can love them, because we dare to be
ourselves in the context of the saving power of God. This is
true not just in individual face-to-face contacts but also as
groups and nations confront one another with great unsolved
political and economic problems crying out for attention.

21

When the Christian faith is so described, several things ought to become clear. First and negatively, Christianity is not a political economy to be established as the alternative to other political and economic schemes. Neither is it meant to be the rationale for a political economy, because it is never a means to some other end. Secondly and positively, since those who claim the faith as theirs are inextricably involved in the political and economic structures of their age —from the patterns of private life to the complex fabric of national enterprise—the Christian faith must enable them to find a sense of meaning and purpose which does not deny or ignore the realities with which they are confronted, but rather offers them a transcendent perspective in which to see the problems of history.

2

OUR TIMES ARE OUT OF JOINT

WHEN THE language of Christian faith is spoken in the modern world, a problem of confused hearing is encountered. There are those to whom it appears to make no sense at all because they think they know what the Christian faith is saying and have decided that it has nothing really important to proclaim to the twentieth-century world. There are those who think of the Christian message in such literal terms that no contact is possible between God's purpose and man's actual situation. In any event, the Christian message is largely understood to be one more of the many voices crying for attention, and to much of the modern western world what it appears to be saying is irrelevant.

Several thinkers have used the phrase "post-Christian" to characterize our age. While the expression can refer to many things, one central note is that there is a prevailing feeling in the modern world that the Christian message has already been spoken and there is nothing further to say. Modern man already knows what it is, and while he may respect the ethical standards derived from the Judaeo-Christian tradition, he does not expect to find any dynamic for his own life from the Gospel as such. This kind of post-Christian is not a casual pagan. He is a serious, responsible person, and his attitude is shared by many people who quite conscientiously carry leadership responsibility in every area of public life. It does no good to suggest that he may be ignorant of the true Christian message, because his original premise is that he knows it. He is aware of anxiety and tension, both in himself and others. He is possibly more sensitive than the average person. But he does not look to the Christian Church for any help.

On the Sunday that President Eisenhower left for the now famous Paris summit meeting (May, 1960), four men played golf in the pouring rain. They were responsible men, quite conscious of the seriousness of the meeting in which President Eisenhower was to participate. They had no pretense of "finding God on the golf course." But they did not expect to get anything from the Church which would speak helpfully to them as they carried a weight of responsibility they could not unload, and therefore they chose another means of helping themselves to live with themselves. These four men only illustrate the way a great many post-Christians feel, and the Church, if it is to fulfill its saving mission, must find a way of speaking its eternal truth so freshly that it can be heard by them.

Regardless of what those who are convinced Christians themselves believe, the fact remains that modern western culture does not so much deny the claims of the faith as rather it refuses to take them seriously. There are two reasons

24

for this. On the one hand, it thinks it understands what Christianity means and feels this to be at best an option and at worst irrelevant. On the other hand, it has many pressing concerns arising out of twentieth-century historical developments, and it does not see how Christianity can speak to these.

If the Christian faith is to become a serious contender for the modern mind, the Church cannot underestimate the importance of the post-Christian attitude. It is not to be answered by shouting it down, but by taking with equal seriousness the problems that conscientious men and women in the secular world are facing. If the problems are real, they must be within the purview of a dynamic faith. Since people are going to have to live with the agenda that history gives them, a faith worth having must, among other things, take the form of power for living in the world that is.

In the light of this observation, the ancient story of the Tower of Babel from the Book of Genesis is a parable quite as descriptive of our times as when it was originally chosen for insertion in the Bible.

"Now the whole earth had one language and few words. And as men migrated in the east, they found a plain in the land of Shinar and settled there. And they said to one another, 'Come, let us make bricks, and burn them thoroughly.' And they had brick for stone, and bitumen for mortar. Then they said, 'Come, let us build ourselves a city, and a tower with its top in the heavens, and let us make a name for ourselves, lest we be scattered abroad upon the face of the whole earth.' And the Lord came down to see the city and the tower, which the sons of men had built. And the Lord said, 'Behold, they are one people, and they have all one language; and this is only the beginning of what they will do;

and nothing that they propose to do will now be impossible for them. Come, let us go down, and there confuse their language, that they may not understand one another's speech.' So the Lord scattered them abroad from there over the face of all the earth, and they left off building the city. Therefore its name was called Babel, because there the Lord confused the language of all the earth; and from there the Lord scattered them abroad over the face of all the earth." (Genesis 11: 1-9)

If the Bible should be thought of as addressed to our culture—our world, our nation, our community, and even our churches—the Tower of Babel story can be seen to point up the fact that the underlying problem of communication is really not one of vocabulary or syntax. It has nothing really to do with the fact that there are different languages spoken by different people, such as English, French, German, Spanish, or Russian. The problem is that we do not hear each other because we are at cross purposes within ourselves, and our own desires and fears speak so loudly that they distort what other people say. We live in a world of competing anxieties, individual and national.

Three Frontiers

In a widely quoted commencement address, Dean Samuel H. Miller of the Harvard Divinity School has described three frontiers which are opening up in our day. He has insisted that the Christian Church cannot fulfill its mission in this mid-period of the twentieth century unless it appreciates the significance of these frontiers in such a way as to make it possible for people to connect their faith with the explorations with which they are confronted. The three frontiers, as Dean

Miller lists them, are: (1) the world of space and speed, (2) the world of the psyche, and (3) the changing nature of the social process. The exploration already going on on all three of these frontiers is being reported back in such a way that it often seems to add to the confusion of our age—hence the challenge to the Christian Church to proclaim its faith relevantly.

When I think of the frontier of space and speed, I not only think of the increasing number of satellites now circling the earth, nor of the experimental flights in man-carrying missiles, such as those performed by Col. John Glenn and Lt. Comdr. Scott Carpenter. Important as is the race between the nations to be the first to place a man on the moon, most people will not be involved in interstellar travel, in the near future at any rate, and these explorations widen our imaginations rather than affect immediately our ways of living. Yet space and speed come closer to home in other ways. Aircraft producers expect to have a Mach-3 (three times the speed of sound) plane ready for commercial use within the next few years, which means that one could fly from New York to London in a little over an hour. When I think of this possibility, I am reminded of the old Polynesian theory that when one travels, it is important to let one's soul keep up with him.

Brown University sponsored a major conference in the fall of 1959 on the subject, "Man's Contracting World in an Expanding Universe," bringing together first-rank speakers from the arts and the sciences, politics, and education. The concluding speaker remarked that the colloquium might have been more aptly named, "Man's Expanding World in a Contracting Universe." Under either title, the issue of the frontier of space and speed is made clear.

27

When we think of the frontier of the psyche, we naturally begin by looking back to the pioneer work of Sigmund Freud in developing the theory of the "unconscious." This concept has proven to be immensely valuable in helping psychiatrists to understand the nature of emotional disorder so that they can guide the patient toward the achievement of a realistic mental health. The theory of the "unconscious" is only one of the ideas contributed by Freud to modern psychotherapy. Without getting into the ideological quarrels between the various psychotherapeutic schools derived from Freud's original work, each of which has built its own distinctive insights into the general understanding of how human personality functions, any serious observer must recognize, first, that the end of this exploration is not in sight, and, second, its influence reaches far beyond the treatment of the emotionally ill. Philosophy, educational theory, and industrial relations are all affected today, in varying degrees, by the need to account for the dynamics of interpersonal relations.

More seriously, many profound and conscientious people find themselves to be conditioned by an understanding of personality which often seems to be at wide variance with the traditional Christian view of personhood. Sometimes this difference of understanding appears to make for irreconcilable conflict—particularly if either side rejects out of hand the integrity of the other at its best. Sometimes the differences are glossed over by verbal definitions that seem to make differing viewpoints come out at the same place so that real issues affecting people's lives are obscured in the interests of making psychiatry and religion happy collaborators. Sometimes efforts are made to make religion an aid to psychiatry with the impression that only the psychiatric orientation matters, or, conversely, psychiatry is viewed only as an aid to the religious interpretation of life. It is not within the province of this book to try to solve the problem of the relationship between the Christian faith and the exploration on the frontier of the psyche. However, it should be observed that both the recognition of conflict and the various attempts to accommodate psychiatry and religion to each other point out the serious importance of this frontier for those who would proclaim the Gospel relevantly to the modern mind.

In any event, exploration will continue on the frontier of the psyche, and the Church cannot proclaim the Christian Gospel as if this did not matter. It is not a question of exploiting this exploration or of being exploited by those whose major interest is in the area of the psyche, but rather of serious conversation with the explorers. Modern depth psychology is a serious discipline, and those who are its disciples need to be understood as being quite as competent within that area as those who have mastered the disciplines of nuclear physics or economics.

When we think of the third frontier—that of the social process—it is important to begin by recognizing certain developments of our times. First, the western world is urban, and urbanization seems to be the price of living on a high technological standard of living. Even where particular families may not actually live in cities, psychological urbanization has marked their lives. Actually there were more people living, at the time of the 1960 census, within the City of New York than on all the farms of America put together. Second, this trend toward urbanization is producing what sociologists call the *megalopolis,* the super-metropolis—great areas with a common economy and transport and distribution of consumer goods. Only a few of these are: from north of Boston to south of Washington; from southwestern Michigan around the end of the lake and north to at least Sheboygan, Wisconsin; and the San Francisco Bay area. Within the *megalopolis,* there is no single center around which life is organized, but rather a plurality of centers with their influence overlapping, and with the same people pulled in various directions by their jobs, their social interests, their churches and other appeals.

Not as much direct exploration has been done on this frontier as on the other two, but at the present time much study is being given to the problem. Even though the Congress has as yet failed to establish a Federal Department of Urban Affairs, it is certain to be created before very long. Any serious consideration of this area indicates that traditional ways of political administration, social organization, and even of parish life within the Christian Church cannot be applied to the modern urbanized world without careful study. The concentration of such tremendous masses of people tends to make the individual feel that he does not count for much—with the twin results of loneliness and irresponsibility. The increasing mobility, particularly of the more highly educated men and women, tends to deprive local communities of effective leadership. Indeed, a basic part of the whole question is whether the term "community" can be given significance in the modern world.

The Problem of Fundamentalism

To much of the modern world the Christian faith seems irrelevant because, on the one hand, many serious people who are willing to admit to both personal and social problems expect little help from the Church, and, on the other hand, pressing demands are arising from exploration on the three frontiers. For these reasons those who are concerned about the Christian Gospel must take the situation seriously.

Before moving ahead to present a possible outline of the way the Gospel can be proclaimed in modern history, it is important to look at the primary disadvantage the Christian Church has in making its message heard. This is the problem of fundamentalism. By fundamentalism, I mean not only the literal acceptance of Bible stories as historic truth, or of creedal statements as if they were newspaper accounts of events, but also the underlying attitude that wants to freeze religion into a hard and fast system, any kind of hard and fast system, under the illusion that life is safer that way. As long as such an attitude prevails, the Church's message can only be one of many voices at the Tower of Babel. It cannot enter into conversation with the explorers on the three frontiers if it is to tell them but not to listen to them. Here are four *fundamentalisms* which seriously handicap the Church's claim to be taken seriously.

The first type of fundamentalism is expressed in the feeling that religion is only one compartment of life, with the rest of experience in one or more other compartments. This assumes that the world can be fragmented, that experience can be fragmented. Therefore, it doesn't really make any difference what a person believes religiously because it does not have anything to do with such areas as engineering, for example. One can be as literal or symbolic about the Bible and the Creeds as he wants to, and indeed standards of orthodoxy can be made to be enforced on other people, so long as one does not have to relate his faith to the meaning of his work, conflicts within the family, or the complex decisions of international life. The Christian faith ceases to be itself when it is made just a compartment of life. It speaks to the totality of experience if it speaks at all.

31

The second type of fundamentalism is expressed in the feeling that religion can be accommodated to the scientific world by watering it down or by making its great affirmations allegorical ways of stating political, economic, or psychological truths. This is an "egghead" temptation, which makes it possible for people with rarefied intellects to carry water on both shoulders and to find something with which they think they themselves can live at the expense of confusing other people. The modern clergyman is particularly tempted by this way of "having his cake and eating it too," by being thoroughly "orthodox" in a way of speaking while being comfortably *au courant* on any of the three frontiers. The Christian faith, however, ceases to be itself when it is accommodated. It speaks to the real world. It does not simply adjust to it.

The third type of fundamentalism is expressed in the feeling that religion in general and Christianity, in particular, can be turned into a simple ethic for family and business. This is the man-in-the-street temptation, because it is much easier to be concerned with what a person ought to do than with what gives meaning and purpose to life. I remember giving the vestry members of the parish I was then serving copies of Canon Theodore O. Wedel's little book, *The Christianity of Main Street,* in which the author tried to point his readers from this simple ethic to the great classical affirmations of the faith. When the men read it, almost with one accord they reported, "Dr. Wedel is attacking what I believe." This type of fundamentalism can be either tremendously respectful or terribly liberal about the Bible and the Creeds because it really doesn't care at all. While the Christian faith results in ethical norms, these are results only. They are not the heart f the matter. In a world crying out for meaning, moral maxims, no matter how sound, are not a faith for living.

The fourth type of fundamentalism is that which with all sincerity is convinced that religion is an aid to some other more important purpose. On the more blatant level, some real estate promoters are said to want a church near, if not a, a new subdivision because this would be good for property values. Several thoughtful people have spoken out on the need for the reunion of Christendom in order that it may more effectively resist communism. Again, this attitude is not really concerned with a faith for life, but in the promotion of some immediate cause. A divided church is an embarrassment both to real estate promoters who don't want to get involved in the rivalries and also to those who wish to pronounce religious sanctions against communism. But important as it may be to have churches near where people live, and important as it may be to contain communism, the Christian faith ceases to be itself when it is used as a means to some other end.

A former student of mine, the Rev. Michael Hamilton, now Episcopal Chaplain at the University of Southern California, wrote the following in *The Church Review* of May, 1960:

'There was a time when I felt that Fundamentalism in either its Biblical or Creedal forms was not too important an evil, but having come in contact with enough students who have either left the Church, or who have avoided it because they thought it encouraged intellectual dishonesty, I have changed my mind.

"As a denomination we must face up to the fact that Biblical literalism makes atheists out of good scientists, and

33

that, while creeds are essential and the best community ex
pression of the core of our faith, they are still provisional.

"A second major problem I have found among Episcopa
lians is that they look on Christianity primarily as trying t
be well-behaved. 'I don't believe Jesus was any more divin
than Buddha or Mohammed,' is a typical theological expres
sion of the negative reaction to this moralism among students
'One man's opinion about religion is as good as another, an
they all add up to the Golden Rule anyway,' is another com
mon attempt to pour oil on these intellectually confuse
waters.

"How far this burdensome concept of obeying selecte
moral teachings is from the exuberant joy of the Apostle
shouting forth the news of the Resurrection of their Lord
soon to be recognized as the Savior of Mankind!"

3

COMMUNITY
AND
CONVERSATION

PEOPLE ARE always seeking to be assured in advance about
the outcome of the problems in which they find themselves.
While there are palmists displaying their signs in every modern city, the kind of assurance that most people are looking
for in our culture is considerably more sophisticated. Often
it is highly scientific. Often it seeks to use the philosophical
heritage of both East and West. Often it seems a rationale in
depth psychology. The fact is, however, that men are always
seeking for some kind of meaning in a world where experience
is not self-explanatory.

In the Gospel of St. Luke, there is a little passage in which
Jesus is asked to authenticate his own mission and he replies
by referring to "The Sign of Jonah."

Now he was casting out a demon that was dumb; when
the demon had gone out, the dumb man spoke, and the

people marveled. But some of them said, 'He casts out demons by Beelzebul, the prince of demons'; while others, to test him, sought from him a sign from heaven. . . . When the crowds were increasing, he began to say, 'This generation is an evil generation; it seeks a sign, but no sign shall be given to it except the sign of Jonah. For as Jonah became a sign to the men of Nineveh, so will the Son of man be to this generation. The queen of the South will arise at the judgment with the men of this generation and condemn them; for she came from the ends of the earth to hear the wisdom of Solomon, and behold, something greater than Solomon is here. The men of Nineveh will arise at the judgment with this generation and condemn it; for they repented at the preaching of Jonah, and behold, something greater than Jonah is here.' " (Luke 11: 14-16, 29-32)

There is no other possibility in history than to read the signs of the times for what they are, to repent of our continual attempts to achieve an unreal security at the expense of responsibility and opportunity, and then to go ahead and do the best we can with what we have where we are, trusting God's love while we do it.

It might be interesting to speculate on the difference between the sign from Jonah and the sign to Jonah; but in both the final point turns on the fact that history offers lessons without guarantees, yet responsible men must learn from what is happening around them if they are going to live effectively where they are and deal conscientiously with the agenda that circumstance places before them. For Jonah, there was no evasion possible—distasteful as the assignment was to preach to Nineveh (as if an American were sent to Moscow) he had to perform it, and he had to learn through bitterness

36

that the Most High God was quite as concerned for the people of Nineveh as for the people of Judah. For those who heard him, there was no other evidence than what they knew about their own lives, but that was enough. In any event, in a world where the future cannot be put on ice, men will never be offered any other sign than the sign of Jonah. The meaning of history, learned from within as we live, is all the sign that we will get.

Abraham Lincoln, in 1862, told a committee of religious leaders who were urging him to free the slaves immediately, 'I hope it will not be irreverent for me to say that if it is probable that God would reveal his will to others on a point so connected with my duty, it might be supposed that he would reveal it directly to me; for, unless I am more deceived in myself than I often am, it is my earnest desire to know the will of Providence in this matter. These are not, however, the days of miracles, and I suppose it will be granted that I am not to expect a direct revelation. I must study the plain physical facts of the case, ascertain what is possible, and learn what appears to be wise and right."

Mr. Walter Lippmann, who does not himself claim a Christian faith, states the issue very clearly in his column of June 3, 1961: "We have had a run of bad news and the time has come when we must make up our minds whether to face it and learn from it, or to shrink from it into a nervous breakdown with suicidal tendencies. There are altogether too many who in dismay and disappointment are ready to admit that Khrushchev is right in predicting that communism is sweeping the world and that, short of war, we have no means of stopping it. They are like the man who . . . is so worried that he will fall off the top floor of the Empire State Building that he stops the elevator and jumps out the ninth-floor win-

37

dow." Mr. Lippmann was, of course, commenting on the American reaction to the world situation, but the tenor of his remarks applies to all other areas of human life where people have to face problems and make decisions without being able to prove in advance that everything will turn out for the best.

In this era of general world uncertainty, it is well to remember what Paul Tillich pointed out in his book, *The Courage To Be*—that the only effective alternative to the Christian faith is Stoicism. It is also well to note that there are many creative and imaginative, not numbly resigned, Stoics who are trying to understand the demands of the modern situation and to respond to them. If the Christian faith is to fulfill its God-given role in these days, it will only be as it is just as intellectually respectable, if not more so, than the best of the Stoics.

Having recognized this, a Christian can now say something more. We not only read the evidence of our times as honestly as we can, because that is all the sign there is, but we also read this evidence in the light of our faith in the God and Father of our Lord Jesus Christ, who works through history and who meets men and women in the actual problem situations of daily life. This in no way minimizes the actual seriousness of the world situation nor the responsibilities of family life. It does not guarantee success on the world's terms but it gives people a different perspective in which to face reality.

Community and Conversation

The Christian Church faces a world which at one and the same time seeks a solution to its problems through human skill and achievement and seeks a sign in the sense of being assured in advance as to the direction events will take. In confronting this world, the Church is both in it and also a community seeking to communicate with it. It is in it in the sense that Christians are necessarily involved in the same historical situation that everyone is. But it seeks to speak to it in the sense that it wishes to enter into a conversation with all who are responsibly concerned about man's welfare.

In the discussion of the third frontier—the changing nature of the social process—in the last chapter, the question was raised as to whether the term "community" could have any precise meaning in modern society. While we must recognize the seriousness of this question both for social planners and for the institutional life of the Christian Church, there is another dimension to the term "community" that needs attention now. The Christian faith always presupposes the existence of the fellowship of God's chosen people, but this fellowship is not dependent for actualization on any particular sociopolitical pattern, least of all town-and-country life of the seventeenth and eighteenth centuries. Community in the sense of the self-conscious association of Christians with each other, taking different forms in different eras, is a necessary part of the Christian proclamation: hence, the affirmation about the Holy Catholic Church in the Apostles' and Nicene Creeds.

The Christian faith will appear irrelevant to the modern world as long as the Church appears to be a "community" where Christians talk only to each other, in the sense of being comfortable solely in exploring the implications of their faith when with other Christians. The Christian faith will appear to be irrelevant as long as the Church, in talking to the secular world, appears to be using clichés when it tries to communicate what it holds to be important. The great terms of the faith were forged in an encounter with reality rather than in ivory tower speculation, but this needs to be spelled out.

When the Church abstracts itself from the world in the interests of more easy dialogue between its members—the perennial temptation of the concerned "core groups" in modern parishes—the result is not a community but a "cultural island." Every family has its "cultural island" aspect where particular words and expressions and even facial grimaces carry meaning which outsiders do not share, but the family to function effectively cannot depend on the intimacies which the members take for granted. It has to be related to the larger social structure in which it is located through work and community activity and even through recreation. In the same manner, the Church is continually asked whether its sense of community is a retreat from reality or rather whether it primarily consists of the development of tools for the general good.

The only sense of community which is worth having, from a Christian point of view, begins with the awareness that Christians are in the same historical situation that everyone else is. The pressures of the international political situation and the uncertainties of the money market affect every man, woman, and child who happens to be alive. The distinctive Christian awareness is that within this historical situation which is recognized for what it is, God makes possible a mutuality of acceptance, forgiveness, and love that empowers people to face reality with utter frankness yet without despair, in the confidence that man has a really creative role to play in the divine scheme of things.

When this is understood, the Christian Church is not a "cultural island" of people talking a kind of private language to each other that has nothing to do with what is going on in the outside world. Rather the Church has something to say to the world as its part of a conversation. The burden of the conversation from our Christian side is that we, under God, are willing to recognize the dynamic nature of sin in history, not just sin in general but our own failures of omission and commission in particular, and above all our continual susceptibility to the temptation to rewrite the rules of life in our own favor. Thus the Church speaks to the world not in indictment but rather as saying something the world really wants to hear. While the world would not use Christian terminology to describe what it is hearing, this is what St. Augustine meant by his phrase, "the good news of original sin."

The Christian Church, in its role of proclaiming the saving Gospel of Jesus Christ to the world, is a community, called into being by the act of God and made up of everyone who accepts for himself a God-given role in the fellowship. This is no "cultural island" of the self-satisfied or the escapists, but rather a community that is willing and ready to enter into conversation with other responsible elements of the world in the common task of making it possible for men and women to live with themselves and with each other within the actualities of history. The Church's function in this conversation is to be self-consciously the community of sinners—forgiven sinners, to be sure—but sinners first of all who are willing to accept what God does in them and through them.

Conversation with the World

If the Christian Gospel is to be proclaimed effectively to the modern world, the Church must be in dynamic conversation with various responsible groups within society. The principle of conversation is most important, because any real conversation is at least a dialogue. It may involve more than two participants, but it does not merit the name "conversation" at all, if it is only a monologue—where one does all the talking and then packs up and goes on to other business without caring about the response. Conversation involves two or more participants who take each other seriously. The Christian Church is the fellowship of those who are convinced that God's saving action in and through Jesus Christ changes the meaning of life for all who come to accept Jesus as Lord. It seeks to be in conversation with individuals and groups who have other serious concerns, which are quite legitimate in their areas of particular competence—politics, economics, psychology, the social sciences, the physical sciences, and the like. Without such a conversation, the world will continue to seek for signs it can never find and to be confused by the babble of many voices.

A conversation not only involves two or more participants who take each other seriously; it involves listening as well as speaking. No conversation is desirable, to say nothing of possible, unless it is assumed by the participants that what the several speakers wish to say is worth listening to. It is not a question of agreement or disagreement, but of realizing that everybody concerned has something to learn. The Christian Church indeed must proclaim "Jesus Christ, the same, yesterday, today and forever"; this does not mean that the Church has nothing to learn about the conduct of its mission through listening to the experience of dedicated people in other areas of life. Here is where the fundamentalist attitude, described in the preceding chapter, is really broken down.

A conversation must have an area of common concern which each participant from his own point of view feels important. The area is the welfare of man, seeking to find meaning and purpose for his life, endlessly looking for an answer to fear, guilt and anxiety. This common concern completes the breakdown of the fundamentalist attitude, because when those who are committed to the Church listen to other responsible people concerned over human welfare from other responsible points of view, there is a real common cause which is worth discussing. While the Church in its loyalty to the Gospel of Jesus Christ must be primarily concerned with man's eternal salvation, this very area of concern itself cannot be abstracted from the other aspects of human life as if one could choose between salvation, on the one hand, and political economy, on the other. While every aspect of experience is ultimately caught up in the Christian understanding of Providence, it is real experience that is so involved— bringing up children, earning a living, living in a neighborhood, organizing a business, casting a vote, paying the income tax, and all the other relationships in which men and women become involved both individually and socially.

A conversation not only depends upon an area of concern common to the speakers, it must also have some conscious awareness of priorities on the part of each speaker. Otherwise there is nothing to share, and the encounter remains at the end precisely where it was when it started. For example, when the Christian Church is in conversation with those who are professionally competent and responsibly involved in urban redevelopment, any effective encounter will depend first of all upon each side having some real convictions as to its own role in the modern world. While those who speak for the Church are not being engaged in responsible conversation if what they are really after is to have the urban redevelopers solve their problems for them (this is exploitation, not conversation), they do have the right to ask the urban planners

43

what they expect of the Church in the community, so that a part of the conversation will take the form of a discussion of the theology of urban redevelopment. It is only through such a process that the Church can communicate an understanding of its own role. But the price of the process is to let the urban redevelopers ask what the Church expects of them, so that they, too, may have part of the conversation take the form of a discussion of the sociology of institutions, both religious and secular.

Finally, an effective conversation demands a reverent agnosticism on the part of each speaker; otherwise, nothing can be learned. The purpose of the meeting is not to make sales, from one side to the other, even though there will be an element of salesmanship where people are seriously convinced of the importance of their interests. The real purpose of the meeting is the discovery of a larger truth than any of the participants know already. It is important for those who are committed to the Christian Gospel to remember that God can speak to them through the action of legislative committees and through the studies of economists and public health workers quite as much as through the Bible and the Creeds. Ultimately, indeed, the message will be the same regardless of the source whence it comes, provided it is in the search of saving truth—but this sameness will not be discovered unless the participants find their own vision wider as a result of their encounter with each other. In *The Flowering of New England,* Van Wyck Brooks said of the people of Boston, "They were willing to learn, provided one admitted how much they knew already." In this kind of dynamic conversation, while mutual respect is indeed a preliminary to an effective interchange, there need be no guarantees in advance.

44

Within this understanding, the conversation can now involve anything that anyone feels to be important for his life. Karl Barth puts the issue in these words:

He [Jesus] asks our young people not about their reports from school, . . . not about their good repute, not even whether parents and pastors are satisfied with them. He asks them about the remarkable dissatisfaction and longing, which disturbs every young person and which is not to be silenced by work or idleness, by obedience or license. . . .

"Jesus asks our wives not about the correctness of their housekeeping and not about the excellence of their qualifications as wives and mothers, but about their fatigue, destitution, and helplessness because they do not know how to accommodate themselves to the lot of womanhood. . . . He asks us men not about our characters, not about our services, not about our activity as professional people and citizens, but about our secret shame, about the wounds of egotism in our conscience, about the open or hidden tragedy of the struggle of our passions with our ideals of righteousness. . . . Jesus asks our pious people not about the state of their conversion and sanctification . . . but about their inward part from which the unredeemed soul cries out: 'I believe, dear Lord, help my unbelief.' "

4

GOD AND THE SEARCH FOR IDENTITY

MODERN MAN is seeking to know who he is. With a poignancy that earlier generations never knew, "the search for identity" has become a major characteristic of our day. While the expression obviously refers to the fact that individual men and women are seeking to discover with some confidence what their own personalities signify, it also can be legitimately used to describe modern society in search of its own soul. At the end of Arthur Miller's play, *Death of a Salesman,* Willy Loman's son speaks at the cemetery, "Dad never knew who he was."

The Christian faith is addressed to this question, but whether or not it can be heard to be saying something which modern man can appreciate is another matter. The First Epistle General of St. Peter has a statement of Christian self-understanding which is either pious gobbledygook or a totally

46

different way of appreciating the meaning of life than the modern world is accustomed to use.

"Blessed be the God and Father of our Lord Jesus Christ! By his great mercy we have been born anew to a living hope through the resurrection of Jesus Christ from the dead, and to an inheritance which is imperishable, undefiled, and unfading, kept in heaven for you, who by God's power are guarded through faith for a salvation ready to be revealed in the last time. . . . Without having seen him you love him; though you do not now see him you believe in him and rejoice with unutterable and exalted joy. As the outcome of your faith you obtain the salvation of your souls. . . . But you are a chosen race, a royal priesthood, a holy nation, God's own people, that you may declare the wonderful deeds of him who called you out of darkness into his marvelous light. Once you were no people but now you are God's people; once you had not received mercy but now you have received mercy." (I Peter 1: 3-5, 8-9; 2: 9-10)

A major difficulty, however, is that the real power of this claim can only be appreciated from within the fellowship. By itself it may appear to offer a promise to the outsider—to indicate a direction in which he may seek for self-discovery through identifying his life with a significant movement. But until he appreciates the context in which the search for identity is dealt with, he can never fully appreciate what the answer is talking about.

The "search for identity" is a major theme in modern psychiatry, with the presupposition that until people get some conviction as to who they are upon which they are willing to live, life will continue to be defeating and pointless. In his thought-provoking novel *Till We Have Faces,* C. S. Lewis has connected the same theme of "the search for identity" to the Christian faith, through the medium of a story about a princess who only dared meet her subjects when wearing a mask. The face behind the mask she felt to be too horrible for anyone to see.

On a New York subway billboard some years ago, I saw an advertisement for a brand of lipstick with the legend, "Date Bait." The suggestion was that it was not the personality of the girl that was important, but rather that her identity was given by the way she decorated her mouth. In the slick magazines, the suggestion is that identity is established by the whisky one drinks, the tailor who makes one's suits, or the photographer who takes one's picture. Only a generation which is partially unsure as to who man is could be influenced very much by such an appeal.

The Bhagavad Gita speaks with a power to convinced Hindus that the western student of the world's religions can never fully grasp even when he appreciates with the utmost sympathy the myth. While we are not concerned here with comparative religion, the illustration from Hinduism should help to make clear that only from within a conscious association with the Christian fellowship can such a passage as that from the First Epistle General of Peter be heard as speaking with power about who men are and what makes life worth living.

As was suggested in the comment on the frontier of the changing social process in Chapter 2, ours is an age when more and more people tend to doubt their own significance as they find themselves tiny unessential residents of gigantic human ant hills. In other words, ours is an age where loneliness in the midst of crowds is on the increase. Is not the inner meaning of loneliness an uncertainty as to who one is and therefore a search for affirmation by other people who are themselves in the same predicament? But the lonely cannot affirm each other. The basic question "Who am I?", which underlies "the search for identity," has no self-evident answer.

My own experience with counselees points up the issue. A counselee will frequently say, "I am beginning to lose my faith." When this is explored, the following syllogism develops in very many instances. The statement really means, "I am beginning to doubt whether there is a god." This turns into, "I am beginning to doubt whether if there is a god, he would care for me." In the last analysis, this turns out to mean, "I do not believe that anyone, god or man, could care for me." Along with the obvious sense of inadequacy underlying such a feeling is a deeper sense of being lost or not knowing who one is in a world which offers few clues.

It is precisely to man's "search for identity" that the Christian faith speaks with confident power.

Identity and Culture

Dr. Paul Tillich once observed that the only time a man is distinctly himself is in choosing with which group to align himself. The search for identity necessarily takes the form of seeking for significant loyalties, because by such a process a person at one and the same time achieves dignity for himself and also points beyond his own self-questioning to something larger, more enduring, more deeply meaningful.

When the political and economic situation appears relatively stable, it is, therefore, very natural for most people to seek to establish their identities in major part by identifying themselves with their culture. This actually means identifying themselves with particular economic, social, political, or ethnic groups within society rather than with the culture as a whole. When the social situation is relatively stable, the groups which comprise society may serve practically as the means through which individual men and women, with particular histories, backgrounds, education, and interests, connect themselves with the way life is being lived around them.

While, as we have seen, all cultures tend to arrogate to themselves the role of religion, in the sense of seeking to provide approved channels in which people will find meaning for their lives, to a certain extent the search for identity within culture is not in and of itself bad. Rather it is not only unavoidable, but within an appreciation of its limits it can be useful. But the ultimate answer to the question "Who am I?" can never be given by the social context in which one lives. In the most tranquil of times, identity established this way is shallow. When the political, economic, and social situation is unsettled, as in the gigantic power struggle on the international level or the mounting racial tension on the domestic scene, the limitations of this approach to the problem of identity are underlined.

There is a great deal to encourage modern men and women to find the answer to the perennial and persistent question "Who am I?" by identifying themselves with American middle-class culture. Indeed, this approach to life has been for the past few decades and continues to be the product the American people as a whole seem to believe they are meant to export to the world. Within American society, the popularity for years of such a book as the late Dale Carnegie's *How to Win Friends and Influence People* (which one of my assistants once paraphrased as "How to Skin Friends and Influential People") actually means taking the cultural presuppositions of American middle-class society for granted and then finding one's meaning by exploiting these presuppositions in personal relationships. The popularity of Dr. Norman Vincent Peale's *The Power of Positive Thinking* and his other books rests upon the assumption that self-fulfillment is possible as the individual accepts the creative achievements of his culture and ignores anything that does not fit in. Even more seriously, the continuation of the movement now known as Moral Rearmament through the various changes of name and "party line" details since the late 1920's is really an attempt to turn American middle-class society, bolstered by an unreal ethical absolutism, into the Kingdom of God in the naive belief that this is all the world needs to overcome the Communist menace.

In his 1960 report to the Trustees of St. Paul's School, Headmaster Matthew M. Warren wrote as follows:

"It has become almost axiomatic that institutions must reflect the immediate concerns of their culture, whether local or national. For institutions to reflect anything other than the culture, and by their very existence to imply judgment on the culture, is insupportable to many citizens. We have adopted in large measure the idea that the culture is self-healing, has self-regenerative qualities and out of its own inwardness is able to make judgments and decisions and develop ways and means of living with itself. We used to smile at the song, 'Fifty Million Frenchmen Can't Be Wrong,' but it is not a laughing matter, when in our own country and under our own processes of development we have come to a place where we think that majorities can make decisions for everybody else, and that often these decisions do not have to be thought out but rather need only the superficial label of 'self-

51

realization.' The result is that self-expression and 'everybody else does' have become new commandments and justify practically anything anyone wants to do. If sloppiness in dress and manner appeal to us at the moment, then neatness and even cleanliness are suspect. If good manners seem troublesome and time-consuming and many people don't want to be mannerly, then rudeness is part of the explanation of its own behavior. This degenerative process will not meet the problems of the day, nor will the fruits of such thoughts stand us in good stead in a time of suffering and darkness and sorrow. We need individualism and independence and freedom, but these marvelously desirable qualities are never far from social life, lawful relationships and order. Order always summons freedom, and freedom resists order, so tension is created; and the individual, the thoughtful individual, lives within the tension and deals with it."

The search for identity within culture necessarily encounters the tension between freedom and order, and it is precisely here that the question becomes serious both for individual men and women and for society. While the modern situation has its own particular ways of experiencing this tension, the whole meaning of identity in any situation is focused by the inner drives to fulfill one's own destiny, on the one hand, and to find an assured place in the social context, on the other. When the Christian Gospel is understood to be speaking to men and women who are seeking to discover who they are in the very conflict between freedom and order, then it can be seen to give meaning to a tension which is otherwise frustrating.

The cultural reaction to the Gospel, however, is simply to take it superficially and to domesticate the Church. Then the

Christian Church is threatened, not so much by hostility from without as from a desire even by its own members to have it taken over by the culture so that it simply becomes an organ of the culture. This would mean that men and women will find their identity, not beyond anxiety, but by accepting with as few questions as possible the norms and criteria which the secular world uses to keep its wheels going round. For thoughtful people, the issue is far from academic, particularly in an era when the explorations on the three frontiers, mentioned in Chapter 2, are changing the familiar landmarks which men and women are accustomed to use in determining where they are, and when the political and economic uncertainties of our age are making many conscientious men and women ask whether there is any point to the continual struggle to make life decent, to say nothing of glorious.

Faith and Identity

The Christian Gospel is directly concerned with the search for identity, precisely because it is directed toward empowering men and women to live creatively and imaginatively as they deal with the actualities of history, knowing that in so dealing they are always in the presence of the God and Father of our Lord Jesus Christ. The third paragraph of the Apostles' Creed, "I believe in the Holy Ghost: The holy Catholic Church: The Communion of Saints: The Forgiveness of sins: The Resurrection of the body: And the Life everlasting," is our cultic way of saying over and over again in the context of worship precisely what the passage from the First Epistle General of Peter is saying. Whenever Christians recite the Apostles' Creed or the Nicene Creed, they are talking about themselves quite as much as they are talking about God;

indeed, unless they know themselves to be talking about themselves, they cannot be talking about God as the Christian faith understands him. For the Creeds are mirrors in which we see ourselves reflected, as it were, in the divine purpose.

The central note of the Christian answer to the search for identity is in the affirmation about the Resurrection—both of Jesus Christ and of ourselves. This was the original proclamation of the early Church, as in Acts 2:36: "God has made him both Lord and Christ, this Jesus whom you crucified." It is only through the Resurrection that there is a new Israel continuing God's saving purpose, but now with the power of forgiveness and new life, in the same old world. It is only through the Resurrection that there is a Church within which living men and women, age after age, in country after country, in situation after situation, can discover and rediscover who they are in God's scheme of things. In making this discovery, they find a meaning and purpose for daily life in the workaday world.

To say the last paragraph of the Apostles' Creed Christianly is to claim an identity, or at least to see a clue to identity, within the fellowship of the Body of Christ. To read the passage from the First Epistle General of Peter in the same spirit is to hear the Word of God telling us the same thing. This does not eliminate the problem of the search for identity as though there were eliminated for good the guilt, the anxiety, and the fear which make men and women again and again question both who they are and whether they are really worth the concern of either God or man. But it provides a context within which this recurring question may be dealt with as it arises. It is in this sense that the preface to the *Sanctus,* which has come down to the modern world with so little change since the earliest days of the Christian era, is so important a part of acting out our identity through receiving Holy Communion:

"Therefore with Angels and Archangels, and with all the company of heaven, we laud and magnify thy glorious Name; evermore praising thee, and saying, HOLY, HOLY, HOLY, Lord God of Hosts, Heaven and earth are full of thy glory: Glory be to thee, O Lord Most High. Amen."

The Church has an answer to the question, "Who am I?" But this is neither an intellectual proposition by itself to be used as alternative to the various statements the world makes about this problem, nor is it a kind of hope that a god in our own image will reaffirm us as we are, in such a way that the questions in our hearts are silenced. The Church's answer is always in the form of a dynamic conversation between God and ourselves. The third paragraph of the Creed and the text from the First Epistle General of Peter describe the context.

What has already been said about the principle of conversation—between the Christian Church and the responsible groups of the secular world—still holds. This is the structure of the conversation in which sensitive people discover God's word addressed to their lives, not only through worship and the Bible and the traditions and statements of the faith, but through the happenings of daily life. Indeed, the more formally religious activities and these daily happenings are supposed to be two sides of the same thing; both are present, regardless of which is uppermost in our minds.

The First Epistle General of Peter speaks of "the holy priesthood," and the function of all priesthood is to mediate— to provide a connecting link between God and man, to intercede for man's insufficiency, and to proclaim God's forgiving, accepting love. To say the Creed or to hear the Word of God in the Epistle is to be directed toward an identity as part of the priestly fellowship, because the Christian Church as a whole serves this purpose of priestly ministration and every man, woman and child has a part. The Epistle tells us that we are "a chosen generation" in the sense that ours is the opportunity now both to be ourselves and to represent God's loving concern for the world to the world. The Epistle says that we are "a holy nation, a peculiar people," in the sense that to find one's identity as a Christian is to be aware of a loyalty transcending but not annulling all the other loyalties we have—to our families, our friends, our businesses, our country. Christians are self-consciously men and women of a double citizenship—not in the sense that a child of British and American parents may hold both citizenships until he is twenty-one when he will have to choose—but in the sense that our paramount loyalty is to be demonstrated through accepting concrete responsibility where we are.

In this sense God speaks to us about who we are through the historical situations in which we find ourselves. He is doing this to everyone, whether Christian or not, but only through identification with the fellowship of which Jesus Christ is Lord can the message be heard with its full clarity. With the note of the Resurrection central in the modern Church, as it was in the first-century Christian fellowship, we hear God stating that sin and death do not have the last word to say about who we are or where we are going. To put the same affirmation in a modern idiom, we dare to believe that anxiety and guilt can be overcome in God's scheme of things, if not in ours.

To find one's identity through claiming membership in the fellowship of the Resurrection is to find life's meaning affirmed. For God, in raising Jesus Christ from the dead, has set a new stamp of value on our lives—in contrast to the world's symbol of the markdown sale, where a commodity is offered at a reduced price, and the tag has the original asking ($10.98, for example) crossed out and a lower figure substituted. But in God's markup sale, we are given a value through being included in the fellowship that represents God's saving purpose for the world. We cannot earn this value any more than we can earn the right to be loved. We are given the value. God opens up new possibilities for us, not just at the end of our lives when we have died, but here and now.

In the third chapter of the Epistle to the Colossians, St. Paul says, "If then you have been raised with Christ, seek the things that are above, where Christ is seated at the right hand of God," and then he goes on to describe how Christians live with each other in the real world of daily experience. We find our identity through the Resurrection right now in this world where people rub elbows with each other and often threaten each other in the process. Even though the times are out of joint, even though many things are confused, even though tremendous question marks lie ahead to be faced, we have a living, dynamic clue as to who we are and where we are going.

At the close of World War II, Bishop Eivand Bergraav, Primate of Norway and hero of his country's resistance to Hitler, visited London. He was taken by the Norwegian Ambassador to England on a tour of some of the bombed-out areas of that great city. As he saw the devastation, the Bishop remarked, "In another war, nothing would be left." Then the Bishop recalls that the Ambassador fulfilled Luther's statement that "every Christian is meant to be Christ to his brother," because he replied, "No, sir, not quite, nothing but eternal life." Everything but God's eternal meaning can be destroyed by human cruelty and error, but there is a meaning and purpose given to us in the Resurrection, and we can identify ourselves with this here and now.

5

THE SAVING PERSON

IF THE CONTEXT in which the Christian seeks most creatively for his identity in these modern days of cultural confusion is by a conscious association with the fellowship of the Resurrection, this itself involves a loyalty to Jesus Christ as Lord, since it is his Resurrection that we share here and now, as we seek to find meaning and purpose for daily life. The two passages from the Epistles of St. Paul, below, both of which deal with the centrality of Jesus Christ as Lord of the lives of faithful believers, mention not the Resurrection, but the Cross. However, the Cross and Resurrection are like the two sides of a coin—inseparable from each other. It is the crucified Christ who is risen. The risen Christ was rejected by men and accepted the Cross trusting in God's love.

When the message of the Cross is heard as the Word of God, spoken to modern men and women about their own lives in the actual situations in which they find themselves, rather than simply as a recollection of the experience of Jesus long ago, then we are confronted by the Saving Person. Indeed, the Christian faith must first be known inwardly rather than as a series of objective propositions about God, man and the universe which a person *ought* to agree with intellectually. Only then can a person understand any dynamic connection between the world in which he lives and God's mighty acts as recorded in Scripture and passed on to modern men and women through the traditions and worship of the Church.

In focussing the Word of God, not simply for the people of first-century Corinth and Philippi, but for all men in all situations all over the globe for all time, St. Paul tells us that life's meaning is to be found only by trusting the saving love of God, as this is revealed through the Cross, even though this seems to be nonsense by the world's normal standards of evaluation. He furthermore tells us that while the Cross has saving power, men and women still have "to work out" their "own salvation in fear and trembling."

"Have this mind among yourselves, which you have in Christ Jesus, who, though he was in the form of God, did not count equality with God a thing to be grasped, but emptied himself, taking the form of a servant, being born in the likeness of men. And being found in human form he humbled himself and became obedient unto death, even death on a cross. Therefore God has highly exalted him and bestowed on him the name which is above every name, that at the name of Jesus every knee should bow, in heaven and on earth and under the earth, and every tongue confess that Jesus Christ is Lord, to the glory of God the Father. Therefore, my beloved,

60

as you have always obeyed, so now, not only as in my presence but much more in my absence, work out your own salvation with fear and trembling; for God is at work in you, both to will and to work for his good pleasure." (Philippians 2: 5-13)

St. Paul tells modern men and women that the Cross is nonsense to the Jew, but he does not simply mean those who accept the official formularies of historic Judaism. Rather he is talking about the psychological Jew, the Puritan, the moralist, the person who is seriously concerned about a just social order. The Cross is nonsense to the Jew because it is immoral. St. Paul, however, reminds us that no matter how high may be our moral ideals, life will never add up to a neat, perfect, moral, equitable balance. This is not a condemnation of the Jew, either historically or psychologically, but rather a reminder that there are limits to man's moral accomplishments. Only the most insensitive reader of modern history would say that the world's plight today is the result of a failure of the nations to aim at great idealistic goals. Rather the plight is the result of failing to understand inwardly the tension between ideals and ambitions, in which every individual and every nation is involved.

"For since, in the wisdom of God, the world did not know God through wisdom, it pleased God through the folly of what we preach to save those who believe. For Jews demand signs and Greeks seek wisdom, but we preach Christ crucified, a stumbling-block to Jews and folly to Gentiles, but to those who are called, both Jews and Greeks, Christ the power of God and the wisdom of God. For the foolishness of God is wiser than men, and the weakness of God is stronger than men." (I Corinthians 1: 21-25)

St. Paul tells modern men and women that the Cross is silly as the Greek mind understands things, but he does not simply mean the popular Greek philosophy of the first century, but rather the rationalist, the scientist, the philosopher, the egghead of all ages. The Cross is silly, and it is unnecessary. It solves nothing. Without depreciating the importance and necessity for careful, analytic thought, measurement, and planning in every area where it can be used, we must remember that there are limits to what can be done with slide rules or syllogisms. God's power through the Cross talks to us not about what things are made of but who we are, and it is concerned with making available the capacity to accept forgiveness so as to be able to forgive and to accept love so as to be able to love.

St. Paul, in the Philippians passage, proclaims the centrality of the Cross from the point of view of Jesus himself rather than from that of the Christian observer. Our part is not to describe analytically what happened on Calvary but to identify ourselves with it. This leads to a strange new attitude toward God, toward other people, and toward one's self, the application of which is in working out our own salvation. Neither St. Paul long ago nor the Church down through the ages has understood the Christian life to be a process of becoming "little Jesuses" in some literal or moralistic sense. Rather what is involved is accepting the Cross as the approach to reality as we encounter reality. The Cross becomes, as it were, a kind of lens through which we see ourselves, our relationships, and the problems which concern us.

The Historic Source and the Living Lord

God's saving conversation with us, which we reflect in our dialogue with the responsible people of the modern world, is both *about* Jesus Christ, his Resurrection and Cross as obverse and reverse of each other, and *through* Jesus Christ. It involves first an historic person who lived at a certain time and place, who did certain things some of which have been recorded for us, and who said certain things some of which have been saved for us, who died on a Cross which he accepted of his own free choice. This conversation involves at one and the same time a living Lord who claims the right to command our loyalty today, not as an elective, not just for those who are inclined that way, not as one of many possible ways of looking at life where one pays his money and takes his choice, but rather as one whose claim upon us is that here and now alone is reality for all men, for all time, in all situations, and there is no alternative.

Ever since the beginnings of modern Biblical scholarship more than a century ago, competent students have been seeking to distill the unquestionably authentic record of things Jesus said and did from the editing and commenting that has marked the New Testament from the time of the first written documents. There is a legitimate task to be done here in seeking to recover the story behind the story in the accounts of the miracles and the apocalyptic statements, and distinguishing between the Synoptic Gospels—Matthew, Mark, and Luke—with their general objective of providing material about Jesus to those who were already committed to him as risen Lord, and St. John's Gospel with its theological interpretation of Jesus as the eternal Christ. But there is a special problem that has to be recognized: to what extent can the student be neutral and objective? Soren Kierkegaard told the story of "the professor" who knew all there was to know *about* the historic Jesus, the passion, and the life of the early Church, and then died quietly in his own bed without ever having become a Christian. The neutral attitude, so necessary for careful scholarship, is always in danger of missing the dynamic which really makes the study worth the effort, while the involved attitude, on the other hand, may easily let loyalty take the place of fact.

It is not within the scope of this book to go further into the issue of Biblical scholarship. It is enough to recognize its important place, and then to state that for the convinced Christian the Jesus of history and the Christ of faith are one and the same. For those who are led to him, as they seek for their own identities in an age when cultural safeguards no longer provide the security they claim, here is a new dimension to reality.

Somehow the two—the historic person and the living Lord —are connected. Somehow the man of Palestine and the Christ of faith are one and the same. The connection is through God's love for us and through us for the world— through God's love for those who identify themselves with the fellowship of the Resurrection and become thereby instrumentalities of the same love reaching out to all those with whom they come in contact. This is the Gospel. Without the Gospel there is no point in theorizing about Jesus, and the students of comparative religion need make no choices for themselves about their own lives. Jesus may be someone else's Christ, but not for the person who does not feel both a sense of identification with the Cross and a sense of mission to the world.

What difference does this make? If it is Gospel—good news about who we are, where we are going, and whether life's struggle is worth the effort—then it makes all the difference in the world. On any other terms, one might as well compare the aphorisms in the Sermon on the Mount with Polonius' farewell advice to Laertes, some of which is sound common sense.

In a little pamphlet entitled, "What Christians Stand For
in The Secular World," published as a supplement to *The
British News Letter* in 1942, the late Archbishop William
Temple wrote as follows: "We must still claim that Christianity enables us to 'make sense' out of the world, not meaning that we can show that it is sense, but with the literal and
more radical meaning of making into sense—what till it is
transformed is largely nonsense, a disordered chaos waiting
to be reduced to order as the Spirit of God gives it shape."

Saved from What and for What?

To talk about Jesus Christ as the saving person suggests
that man needs saving. If this is coupled with the universal
aim of the Gospel, then it means that every man, woman,
and child who will ever live will need saving. The Christian
faith is built upon the presupposition that Jesus' act on the
cross was not simply for himself but for us, and through us
for all men, for all time. The question then is: saved from
what and for what?

Much of modern drama harps on the problem of man's
inability to love and let himself be loved. In T. S. Eliot's *The
Cocktail Party,* Cecil says, "Hell is being alone." Or again,
in Tennessee Williams' *Cat on a Hot Tin Roof,* Brick says to
Big Daddy, ". . . things, things, things, all these things . . .
but you never gave me love."

Saved from what?—from isolation. Loneliness in the last
analysis is the best clue there is to the meaning of *sin.* Behind circumstantial loneliness—the fact that no one else happens to be around, and there is a lot of circumstantial loneliness in modern urban society—is this profound sense of
isolation from meaningful relationships. Man's own problem
becomes, as it were, the universe of his concern, and every-

thing else is out of focus. One time my son accidentall
slammed the car door on my thumb, and for a week or so
was really a sore thumb with a man attached. The pain an
the difficulty of doing things became the universe of concern
in large measure, and eventually the experience became a
eye-opener as to the deeper meaning of isolation—where ou
own problem is primary, and everything else including thos
who want to love us is secondary.

Here is Paddy Chayefsky in *The Tenth Man* having on
of his characters, Arthur, say to The Girl: "Life is utterl
meaningless. I have had everything a man can get out of lif
—prestige, power, money, women, children, and a handsom
home only three blocks from the Scarsdale Country Club, an
all I can think of is I want to get out of this as fast as I can."

In his little book, *The Great Divorce*, C. S. Lewis gives
picture of hell in the form of a bus trip in the course of whicl
people grow farther and farther apart and littler and little
until all possibility of contact is lost. In the final circle o
The Inferno, Dante gives us a picture of lost souls, immo
bilized and eternally isolated in a world of ice. This is a pic
ture of unredeemed loneliness, unredeemed because in th
last analysis the people involved do not want it to be re
deemed or are afraid to risk the chance.

To appreciate what salvation means requires, first of all
seeing that reality has a triangular shape, without which ther
is no way for personality to be connected with history. Th
Gospel does something to this triangle, but the triangle i
there beforehand. The three angles are: (1) me, (2) societ
—either other individuals or people in groups, or mankind a
a whole, and (3) the universe, the totality of that which is. I
one of the angles is left out, the picture of reality is untrue—
man simply cannot live with other people in a world where h

66

gnores the facts of gravity, light, heat, cold, space, time, death, etc. Neither can man live by adjustment to reality as if there were no other people in the world, because every encounter with other people involves, at least implicitly, both threat and opportunity—the threat that I will be exploited, and the opportunity to exploit—regardless of the sentimentality with which this is felt. Of course, the primary angle, I or me, cannot be left out, or there is nothing to discuss.

What the Christian faith does is to place the Cross—the Cross of Christ, which we dare to accept as our own by claiming him as Lord—at the center of the triangle. Until our appreciation of reality is transformed by the Cross, we cannot help but live in a fragmented world, where people are always trying to doctor the picture of reality in order to avoid anxiety and to fulfill what they take to be their own destinies. Individuals do this and groups and nations do this. The universe is at best natural law which can be understood to a certain extent and even used—the way the principle of an airplane wing does not cancel the law of gravity but overcomes it by compressing air under the wing, through the forward motion of the plane and the wing's shape. Human relations may be humanitarian and benevolent, but there can be no principle of self-criticism which has validity because there is no point of reference beyond what seems to work. Therefore, it is no wonder that loneliness is chronic, because along with self-consciousness comes a sense of isolation.

When the Christian faith places the Cross at the center of the triangle, then the meaning of all three angles is transformed. I am no longer a self-conscious isolate, but know myself to be loved as a child of God, given the value mark of the Cross. Other people—individuals, groups and mankind in general—become, potentially, the family of the children of

67

God, where meetings, instead of being threats and opportunities for exploitation, become occasions for harmonious interaction. The universe is no longer impersonal force and natural law but the expression of the Creator-Father's will. Indeed, there can be no Christian doctrine of Creation at all until the Cross is at the center, because Creation is not so much an account of causality as it is of meaning. The Epistle to the Hebrews sums up what this transformed triangle means in the passage, "We see not yet all things put under his feet, but we see Jesus." Not everything is straightened out, in the sense of eliminating problems and questions, either in self-acceptance or in relationship to God's creation or in interpersonal contacts. But there is a dynamic context given in which men and women may "work out" their "own salvation with fear and trembling."

Saving Action

The Saving Person does not deal with our brokenness, our loneliness, by giving us more law—things we ought to do to make us feel that much the more guilty. This would just add to the problem rather than heal it. He meets us through saving action.

The heart of the Gospel is not the familiar two commandments of Jesus: "Thou shalt love the Lord thy God with all thy heart, with all thy mind, with all thy soul, and with all thy strength," and "Thou shalt love thy neighbor as thyself." The heart of the Gospel is reflected in St. John's proclamation, "For God so loved the world that he gave his only Son, that whoever believes in him should not perish but have eternal life"—eternal life here and now. St. Paul puts it in these words, "For God commends his love to us, since while

we were yet sinners, Christ died for us." For those who can
relate themselves to God's love through the Saving Person,
the two commandments become guidelines toward working
out salvation with "fear and trembling." Otherwise, they are
occasions for more loneliness, more isolation, the result of
more guilt.

Once the triangular view of reality makes sense, loving
one's neighbor as one's self becomes possible, because one
now has a self worth loving. Man cannot really love unless he
knows himself to be loved, and it is this loved self that is
now able to reflect love outwardly to others. Our human experience gives an insight into what is meant by this and also
shows us the limitations to human loving. But what people
cannot do, God does, and this is the way the world was
designed to be.

In the old *Boy Scout Handbook*, there was a description
of the emergency treatment of snake bite. The one who was
trying to help made a cut in the form of a cross at the place
the fangs went in, and then sucked out the poison with his
mouth. Is it too fantastic to think of the saving act of the
Cross as Jesus drawing into himself the loneliness, the anxiety,
and the guilt of the world, so that men and women might be
able to live in a transformed reality?

The Saving Person takes people who often feel unaccept-
able, and makes them know that they are accepted by God
for who they are, without illusions yet with great expectation.
The Saving Person takes people who often feel that they are
unforgivable, who cannot forgive themselves for their failures,
and embraces them with the forgiveness of a God who still
has a place for them in his saving scheme for the world. The
Saving Person takes people who are sure that they are un-
lovable, who are convinced that if anyone really knew them

69

as they know themselves, he would not abide them for a moment, and marks them with God's value mark in order that they become channels for love to enter human history.

This is the saving act of the Gospel, as Jesus Christ becomes Saving Person. Yet one more thing has to be said. It is far easier to explain this conviction in words and to urge other people to lay their anxieties at the foot of the Cross than it is to do so one's self. I have my moods when I know that I can preach "justification by faith"—trusting God's saving love despite human insufficiency—to everybody but myself. My continual human inclination is to want some more tangible assurance of my value, whether in the form of money, power, or prestige. In other words, one may learn what the Christian faith says and be sure that this is right, but living it day in and day out is something else again. Every man and woman who has any honest realism knows that doubts and uncertainties are not blotted out so they never recur, but the Gospel is proclaimed precisely to those who are never excused from the task of working out their own salvation.

The Saving Person meets me in my doubt as well as in my guilt and still accepts me—not giving me answers, but rather his supporting presence. This is why I repeatedly need a personal Savior and not just the understanding of a saving principle. This is why the Cross of Jesus Christ is offered to me in my confusion and to all humanity in our modern confusion. Life will never be cut and dried, but it can be lived.

6

THIS PURPOSEFUL UNIVERSE

"IN THE BEGINNING God created the heavens and the earth. The earth was without form and void, and darkness was upon the face of the deep; and the Spirit of God was moving over the face of the waters. And God said, 'Let there be light'; and there was light. And God saw that the light was good; and God separated the light from the darkness. God called the light Day, and the darkness he called Night. And there was evening and there was morning, one day. . . . Then God said, 'Let us make men in our image, after our likeness; and let them have dominion over the fish of the sea, and over the birds of the air, and over the cattle, and over all the earth' . . . So God created man in his own image, in the image of God he created him; male and female he created them. And God blessed them, and God said to them, 'Be fruitful and multiply, and fill the earth and subdue it; and have dominion over the fish of the sea and over the birds of the air and over every living thing that moves upon the earth'. . . . And God saw everything that he had made, and behold, it was very good." (Genesis 1: 1-5, 26-29, 31a)

"In the beginning was the Word, and the Word was with God, and the Word was God. He was in the beginning with God; all things were made through him, and without him was not anything made that was made. In him was life, and the life was the light of men. The light shines in the darkness, and the darkness has not overcome it. . . . And the Word became flesh and dwelt among us, full of grace and truth; we have beheld his glory, glory as of the only Son from the Father. . . . And from his fullness have we all received, grace upon grace. For the law was given through Moses; grace and truth came through Jesus Christ. No one has ever seen God; the only Son, who is in the bosom of the Father, he has made him known." (John 1: 1-5, 14, 16-18)

These are very familiar passages. The Genesis passage is in the form of a poem with a refrain to each stanza, "God saw what he had made, and behold it was good." Through this ancient poetic description of the beginning of all things, we hear the Word of God describing, not causality, but meaning. The raw material of this universe is essentially good. It is what men do with it that raises problems. There is nothing wrong with the study of psychology, both of individuals and of society, but the term "Madison Avenue" suggests a moral question with regard to its use. Is it to help people understand better what their needs are and how to meet them or to exploit people by playing upon their weaknesses in order to stimulate them to buy products? It is very interesting that many of the physicists who had worked on the early phases of the atomic bomb rediscovered the moral dimension to science in their own reaction to Hiroshima and Nagasaki. The raw material of this universe is essentially good—this is the Christian understanding, particularly in the triangular view of reality with the Cross at its center. All creation is good—whether we are thinking of this earth or of the moon or of Venus or Mars. The astronauts don't change this in the slightest.

The St. John's Gospel passage assumes what Genesis says, that the raw material of the universe is good, but it goes further. Man has freedom to make significant choices, and his decisions matter, but he is not left alone to sink or swim. Grace is the Biblical word describing God's loving outreach to people where they are. Grace and truth are, through Jesus Christ, not as a divine afterthought but as the very heart of the cosmic process. This is a statement of what is central in the divine scheme of things, and to hear it as the Word of God addressed to us where we are means to discover that we, too, are involved in the divine scheme of things.

The two passages together point up the Christian faith: that we who find God confronting us where we are through the events of daily life and the developments of history, and who also discover the saving fact of the Cross-Resurrection as something that not only describes Jesus but also refers to us, know that total reality is shot through with meaning. The explorations on the three frontiers in no way threaten this meaning; they rather enlarge it and deepen it.

"Reality" is a term which everyone uses and few define. In this book, it is used to refer to what we might call the *is-ness* of things. If we were being technically philosophical, we might use the words "essence" or "ontology." It seems obvious to say that that which is is, but it is exactly what is

73

meant. The physical world is as physical scientists show it to be, and while they may learn new understandings about it, and we will then have new insights into this aspect of reality, it will still be true that that which is is. There will be, in a sense, much more to it. While it is sometimes necessary for scientists, in order to be precise, to distinguish between (1) demonstrated facts, (2) axioms, and (3) working hypotheses, it is not necessary for the average man and woman to worry too much about this side of the matter. That which reputable scientists believe can be trusted until they correct their beliefs with new discoveries. But what we do with the results of these inquiries, both in international affairs and domestic policy, raises long-range moral questions.

In the same manner, reality includes the insights of the social scientists—the sociologists, the economists, the political scientists, and the psychologists. Again, it is important for them to distinguish between what are statistical norms and what are demonstrable facts (no individual Vassar graduate actually has two and a half children), and perhaps the layman should be a little more knowledgeable in his own self-defense. Nevertheless, to the extent that insights in the social sciences are accurate and demonstrable, they must be taken seriously until they are corrected by new and better insights.

Again, the psychic world is as it is. The insights of the psychotherapists, and particularly of the dynamic schools of analytical psychology, have given us new understandings of how personality operates in relationships with other personalities. People may go overboard and "psychoanalyze" themselves and their neighbors, or in reaction they may try to reject depth psychology as nonsense. Nevertheless, there are insights into reality which need to be taken seriously. As a more mature popular appreciation of what this means de-

74

velops, some changes may become necessary in the way family and business are handled. In any event, we are not changing the universe but only understanding more about it.

The doctrine of the Trinity is the way the Christian faith understands the triangular nature of reality, with the Cross at the center, and seeks in the light of that Cross to connect faith and experience. The underlying religious question is not really where did things come from nor how do they work, but rather do they make any difference to life's meaning.

God, the Father-Creator-Redeemer

While there is much to suggest that we are mere flotsam and jetsam on a sea of circumstance, whether we are studying microphysics or astronomy or the social process or reading the news of the day, Christians do not ignore the evidence that suggests this. Rather they seek to face it as honestly as possible, admitting their own doubts. But through the grace of God they dare to see beyond it. Creation is the Christian answer to the world's purported meaninglessness. Our dynamic conversation with God—the Cross-Resurrection as one side and our own experience as the other—gives us a new way of looking at life, a new perspective on the same facts, but the facts are still there. Because of Christ we are able to say, "This is within the providence of God, the Father-Creator-Redeemer."

It is basic Christian conviction that no conceivable scientific discovery, not even the synthesis of life, such as seems to be likely within the next few years through the use of the amino acids, will destroy what is truly Christian faith. No new psychotherapeutic insight, nor developments in the fields of politics and economics, nor the planting of a colony of earthmen on the moon will change this central Christian conviction. Even if men should be produced from the test tube, they will still need converting. If man develops the capacity to explore interstellar space, he will still need the Saving Person. When men finally land on the moon or one of the planets, and even if they discover forms of life different from what we know, the grace of God will still be there.

In prophetic lines, the late Dean Howard Chandler Robbins of the Cathedral of St. John the Divine, wrote in 1932:

> "And have the bright immensities
>   Received our risen Lord,
> Where light-years frame the Pleiades
>   And point Orion's sword?
> Do flaming suns his footsteps trace
>   Through corridors sublime,
> The Lord of interstellar space
>   And Conqueror of time?
>
> "The heaven that hides him from our sight
>   Knows neither near nor far:
> An altar candle sheds its light
>   As surely as a star;
> And where his loving people meet
>   To share the gift divine,
> There stands he with unhurrying feet;
>   There heavenly splendors shine."

When we talk about God, the Father-Creator-Redeemer, we are talking at the same time about ourselves, about who we are. This is the answer to the sentimentality so current in our culture about the infinite value of human personality, as if there were something intrinsically significant about the human race just as human race. It is the love of God that makes human personality valuable, that gives value to my life. What ties me to my brother is my conviction that Christ died for him quite as much as for me, so that together we are in the same family. When we say God the Father-Creator-Redeemer we are at one and the same time affirming a value for our own lives and a value for our brothers' lives, regardless of race, color, language, or background.

One cannot speak of God the Father in a Christian sense if his life is lived on the premise that he is the only child. Much in the modern world suggests that life is held rather cheaply; but the Christian faith stands in sharp contrast, not because of a different theory, but because God has acted in his world and continues to act through us. Lewis Mumford in one of his books remarked about the difference in the general attitude between the Zabern incident of 1913, when a tremendous international protest was provoked because a Prussian officer struck a lame Alsatian cobbler with his sword, and this post-World War II era, when genocide has been proven possible and the mass destruction of civilians has been military strategy. But whether life has become cheaper or dearer as the nations deal with people, when Christians say God the Father-Creator-Redeemer, they are responding to a different system of values. The Cross-Resurrection is God's saving act for my life, and by the same token I belong to a family. Our value as human personalities is given by the divine scheme of things.

The Love of God

The central aspect of reality, once we speak of a created universe, is not the speed of light—186,000 miles a second

—important as is the speed of light for astrophysics and for experiments with nuclear energy. The central aspect of reality, once we speak of a created universe, is not gravity —neither Newtonian nor Einsteinian—important as is an understanding of gravity for appreciating the way energy, mass and matter operate. The central aspect of reality, once we speak of a created universe, is not the principles of thermodynamics, as defined or refined in our day by nuclear science, important as it is to appreciate the way matter turns into energy. The central aspect of reality, once we speak of a created universe, is not in Heisenberg's principle of indeterminancy, even though some naive theologians would like to exploit this to authenticate free will. Yet it is still important to know that there are infinite variations possible in predicting the behavior of an electron. The central aspect of reality is not even in the unconscious mind, important as this is for understanding human personality.

The central aspect of reality, once we speak of a created universe, not just a universe that exists but a created universe, is God's love for us. This is more basic than the speed of light, the laws of gravity, or the principles of thermodynamics and indeterminancy, more significant than the unconscious mind and the psychic interaction between creativity and sexuality. Of course, serious and responsible people will not ignore these aspects of reality, but rather they will see them in a new light. Our value is placed beyond any possible impeachment by the act of the Almighty through Jesus Christ our Lord.

The doctrine of Creation will come in for new study and new popularity in the days ahead because it enables men and women to make sense out of much that is otherwise nonsense. For nearly 150 years, it did not really make much sense for

78

most people, because it was used as an alternative explanation for anthropology and geology. Christians today know, however, that a competent geologist must be taken seriously in his own field and that the history of civilizations can help us understand our own society. But the doctrine of Creation primarily concerns value. It concerns God and men and the relationship between them—Father-and-son, Father-and-family, the triangular picture of reality with the Cross at its center.

The Love of God, taken as the central aspect of reality, means, therefore, something more immediate and more practical than that there is no essential contradiction between Christian faith and the explorations on the three frontiers. While the word "love" itself has a variety of meanings, the note of concern for the person who is loved goes through all of them. In our imperfect and distorted human experience of loving and being loved, we know what it is to worry because someone we love is worried and to rejoice because we share the joy of a beloved. This is a clue to what Christian conviction affirms. When we say that the Love of God is the central aspect of reality, we are saying by the same token that man's fears and griefs, his anxieties and guilt, and his joys and achievements are all significant in the divine scheme of things.

As Francis Thompson has put it:

> "O heart I made, a Heart beats here for thee,
>   Face My hands fashioned, see it in Myself;
>   Thou hast no power nor canst conceive of Mine
>   But Love I gave thee with Myself to love
> And thou must love Me, who have died for thee."

Again, when we say that the Love of God is the central aspect of reality we are going further than saying that God is concerned about the total persons we are. Love by any definition involves mutuality. There is no point in simply saying theoretically that the Love of God is the central aspect of reality, unless this suggests that we can return that love. As St. Augustine, who so well understood the basic religious issue, stated, "Thou hast made us for Thyself, O Lord, and our hearts are restless until they find their rest in Thee."

Since the triangular picture of reality with the Cross at the center is that which makes clear the fact that the Love of God is the central aspect of reality, it will follow that God will use me to love other people and, by the same token, he will use other people to love me. While the love relationship between God and the individual man is not confined to situations which involve third parties, it will not ring true if third parties are left out very long. Indeed, it will not ring true very long if it is only limited to what we do benevolently for others. Is not the most gracious of God's gifts perhaps the capacity to let other people love us and to receive gratefully what is offered?

The doctrine of the Holy Spirit is the way the Church has understood God's love to be operative in human relationships, particularly in, but not limited to, the fellowship of those who share a common Christian faith. In this light, it becomes clear that Church and Mission must be part and parcel of each other; Church without Mission is simply self-satisfied sect not worthy of the name of Christ, and Mission without Church to include everyone in fellowship can become spiritual imperialism.

7

OUR ONGOING MISSION

THE CONCEPT of the City of God in contrast to the city of this world has been used over and over again. Probably the most famous is St. Augustine's *City of God,* written in an age of political, economic, and social crisis, the seriousness of which was brought home to the entire Mediterranean world by the news of the fall of Rome. The symbol of the City of God was also used by John Bunyan in *Pilgrim's Progress,* which was until recently one of the most widely read and influential books in the English language. The idea of "city" suggests people in harmonious relationship with each other rather than simply individual perfection, and it implies that the triangular description of reality which has been dealt with in the last two chapters somehow comes into its own in God's fulfillment of his divine purpose.

Dr. Walter Russell Bowie puts the point as follows:

81

"O holy city, seen of John,
    Where Christ, the Lamb, doth reign,
Within whose four-square walls shall come
    No night, nor need, nor pain,
And where the tears are wiped from eyes
    That shall not weep again!

"O shame to us who rest content
    While lust and greed for gain
In street and shop and tenement
    Wring gold from human pain,
And bitter lips in blind despair
    Cry, 'Christ hath died in vain!'

"Give us, O God, the strength to build
    The city that hath stood
Too long a dream, whose laws are love,
    Whose ways are brotherhood,
And where the sun that shineth is
    God's grace for human good.

"Already in the mind of God
    That city riseth fair:
Lo, how its splendor challenges
    The souls that greatly dare—
Yea, bids us seize the whole of life
    And build its glory there."

The Christian finds a transforming faith to enable him to live with the contrast between life as God has designed it to be, as this is revealed through the Person of Jesus Christ, through the Bible, through the traditions of the Church, and as this is reiterated dramatically in the liturgy, and life as we experience it in our self-consciousness and in our awareness of what is going on in the world around us and as we participate in it ourselves. This transforming faith is given us by the Saving Person, and sustained by the ongoing experience of the fellowship of the Resurrection. We find ourselves living in a universe which has dimensions to it that the secular world can never appreciate, as we find ourselves engaged in a dynamic conversation with God and with other people in the presence of the Christ, whose Cross is shared with us.

"Then I saw a new heaven and a new earth; for the first heaven and the first earth had passed away, and the sea was no more. And I saw the holy city, new Jerusalem, coming down out of heaven from God, prepared as a bride adorned for her husband; and I heard a great voice from the throne saying, 'Behold, the dwelling of God is with men. He will dwell with them, and they shall be his people, and God himself will be with them; he will wipe away every tear from their eyes, and death shall be no more, neither shall there be mourning nor crying nor pain any more, for the former things have passed away.' And he who sat upon the throne said, 'Behold, I make all things new.' Also he said, 'Write this, for these words are trustworthy and true.' And he said to me, 'It is done! I am the Alpha and the Omega, the beginning and the end. To the thirsty I will give water without price from the fountain of the water of life.' . . . And I saw no temple in the city, for its temple is the Lord God the Almighty and the Lamb. And the city has no need of sun or moon to shine upon it, for the glory of God is its light, and its lamp is the Lamb. By its light shall the nations walk; and the kings of the earth shall bring their glory into it, and its gates shall never be shut by day—and there shall be no night there; they shall bring into it the glory and the honor of the nations." (Revelation 21: 1-6, 22-26)

And as we hear the passage from the Revelation of St. John the Divine as the Word of God addressed to us where we are, as the latter half of the twentieth century is grinding out its troubled story, we know that Christian confidence is not in man's success but in God's ultimate victory, of which men can be agents. In the eighth chapter of the Epistle to the Romans, St. Paul says, "We know that all things work together for good to them that love God." He does not mean that the pious will get the breaks in the way their fortunes turn out, which is obviously untrue historically. He does mean that those who love God, who are oriented to the triangular view of reality with the Cross at the center, are able to discern a meaning in history where the world sees only confusion.

The Christian Faith Lived in History

To know ourselves to be in dynamic conversation with God in the fellowship that is called into being by the Resurrection of Jesus Christ the Lord is to know that in some tangible way this same Jesus Christ is Lord both of our private lives and of the fortunes of the nation. By the same token, it is to know that we have a mission in his name to the world he came to save. And this mission is to do what we can, as best we understand it, where our influence can count, to conform individual and social life to the divine purpose.

When people first get an inkling that mission is what is involved in living the Christian faith in history, they often feel that they ought to take on some kind of professional church work on a full-time basis. One of the tragedies resulting from an ineffective proclamation of the Gospel is that a

84

vital ministry of the laity is something about which most church members have never heard. Therefore, when a man discovers the urgency of the Christian faith for his own life, he is often tempted to resign whatever is his present vocation and study for Holy Orders, or, even more sadly, to feel that since he is too old or has too heavy obligations to make this transfer, he is somehow lost. The organized life of the Church needs a ministry of the laity which has integrity in its own right and is not simply a kind of carbon copy or pale imitation of what clergymen do. To know the Christian faith as one's own does involve a sense of mission, but for most people this will not be in the form of professional church work.

A responsible sense of mission necessarily has to be connected in some way to the ongoing life of the Christian fellowship, but it does not mean that any particular form of the Church's institutional life, as we know it, need necessarily survive or, indeed, ought to survive. Much of Protestant parish life in America, for example, is actually an adaptation of the pattern of agricultural villages, each with its church at the center, that obtained in the Middle Ages. This has been transformed by, first, the industrial revolution and, second, the development of the modern suburb, not into something which is particularly functional in terms of the crying needs of society but rather into a religious club providing chaplaincy services and sponsorship for activities. A sense of mission will, indeed, need to be related to the ongoing life of the Christian fellowship, if it is to be responsible rather than sentimental, but perhaps this calls for exploration on still another frontier.

The Christian faith is lived in history through a sense of mission, and four areas in particular cry out for its outreach

—family life, the meaning of work, race relations, and the international order. In every instance, a responsible sense of mission necessarily includes taking seriously the technical disciplines involved in each area of concern, and recognizing that there are power structures in each area which cannot be ignored.

The great need in family life is for people who want to love each other and to be loved by each other to be able to communicate with each other, but so often communication becomes merely the exchange of information about externals rather than heart talking to heart. When a teenage boy or girl says to a parent, "You don't understand what I mean," he is not suggesting that the adult does not comprehend the dictionary meaning of the words he is using, but rather that the generations live in different worlds. It is not a question of who is wrong or right, but of failure to be able to meet significantly. When a woman says, "Wait till I put on my face," she is saying that she is not comfortable in speaking until she is playing a role, and even the closest husbands and wives fail to escape acting parts with each other rather than being fully themselves. Here is an area in which all living people, even single persons, share indirectly and which provides the day-to-day framework for living, but without communication there is confusion and frustration as well as fulfillment and joy. The mission to family life is directed to making it possible for husbands and wives, parents and children, to appreciate each other's personhood within the triangular view of reality with the Cross at the center.

The great need in the area of work is that while every living person is involved, the problem of meaning is far from clear. Indeed, the modern confusion over what to do with

86

retirement suggests that there is a lack of clarity as to the meaning of the work from which people are forced to retire. When Eli Whitney developed the theory of interchangeable parts—actually a much more revolutionary invention than the cotton gin—he made possible assembly-line production and our present high standard of living. But part of the price that the modern world has paid for standard brands and standard gadgets is in the form of standardized employees, whether at a bench or at a desk, regardless of the level of responsibility and pay. Standardization does help to clarify job specifications, but there is a side to man that cannot be taken care of in this way without becoming less than personal. Work is meant to be something more than the process by which individuals and families acquire purchasing power with which to satisfy their other needs. In God's providence, it should have some meaning in its own right. The mission to the area of work is directed toward helping people put this most basic aspect of their own self-understanding and of their relationship with other people—employees, employers, fellow employees, customers, salesmen, etc.—within the triangular view of reality with the Cross at its center.

The great need in the area of race relations is for people with different ethnic and cultural backgrounds to be able to meet each other as fellow children of God for whom Christ died rather than as members of a hostile bloc to be resisted, or exploited, or kept in place, or overcome. The clash between Negro aspirations for full citizenship and the southern tradition of white supremacy is the most obvious but not the only area of interracial tension in America; it certainly is not the only one in the world. They all originate in the fact that identifiable minorities, whether ethnic or linguistic or cultural, tend to cause suspicion and fear and are easily used as scapegoats. In a symbolic expression, Jacques Maritain has said that it is the historic role of Israel to be the continual sensitizer of the conscience of mankind, because the Jew is always a minority, and by the Jew's very existence he is asking Gentiles whether they really believe the ethics they profess. The mission to race relations is directed toward making it possible for people to recognize personhood over and beyond identifiable differences, because within the triangular view of reality with the Cross at the center men are racially colorblind and all speak the same language.

The great need in international life is for men to develop ways of channeling the terrific power they have developed for exerting political pressure so that they can work through the various problems which keep the nations anxious. Is the expression "the cold war" actually descriptive of international normality, or is it a serious disease somehow to be brought under control? There is terrible responsibility laid upon the leaders both of the United States and Russia in these days when the world's political power is polarized between Washington and Moscow, and this has to be taken seriously. The ideological clash between Democracy and Communism makes the situation that much more urgent. The mission to international relations is certainly not to propose that the Sermon on the Mount be substituted for diplomacy. But it is directed toward helping both those who make policy and those who comprise the public to recognize that while we must maintain what we believe to be right, as we seek to establish international peace and justice, still God's ultimate concern for human society cannot be fulfilled in any existing or projected system.

The Christian Faith Transforming History

To know ourselves in dynamic conversation with God and other people from within the triangular view of reality with the Cross at the center is to recognize that the Christian faith in a real way transforms history. This is in radical contrast to the cultural view that has prevailed for the past two or more centuries: that somehow progress is automatic, and all change is for the better, in the long run if not immediately. Rather, historic change—in the political and economic structure, in the social process, and in the results of explorations on the three frontiers—is always a widening of the possibilities within which significant decisions are possible. The Christian view of historic change likewise avoids the cynicism implied in the old French proverb: *"Le plus ça change, le plus la même chose"* (the more it changes, the more it is the same thing). While the problem of human sin will continue to be a factor in all serious decision making regardless of what developments occur in history, the accomplishments of men and nations are real and the stage for our decisions is altered.

The Christian faith transforms history, beginning with our understanding of who we ourselves are. Dr. William C. Menninger, of the Menninger Psychiatric Foundation, has written interestingly on the importance of building what he calls "ego strength" for mental health. Without going into detail as to what is implied in the expression "ego strength," mental and spiritual health mean that persons are not at basic cross-purposes within themselves and that, therefore, they can accept reality for what it is. In Soren Kierkegaard's book, *Purity of Heart Is to Will One Thing,* there is the image of a lake. Kierkegaard says that when the wind blows across the lake, the surface is broken up into myriad little mirrors, all set at different angles, and the result is a confused and distorted reflection of the hills and the sky. But when the lake is calm, it is like a single mirror giving a clear, exact reflection. While as long as human nature lasts, men and women will have conflicting desires and fears, and the world will continue to offer confused problems demanding action, the Christian can accept this and live with it. Therefore, he is not the victim of history, but shares in principle God's mastery of history.

The Christian faith likewise transforms history in the way it affects our relationships with other people. In the Epistle to the Galatians, St. Paul says, "For as many of you as were baptized into Christ have put on Christ. There is neither Jew nor Greek, there is neither slave nor free, there is neither male nor female; for you are all one in Christ Jesus." St. Paul is going behind the rite of Holy Baptism to the kind of relationship that Christian loyalty understands to be God's purpose for his children. Differences will continue to exist and will be important. Indeed, as St. Paul himself must have known in referring to "male and female," some differences are essential. The Christian faith does not annul man's distinctiveness, as if each person had the same I.Q. that everyone else has, as if sex no longer mattered, and as if power structures of one kind or another were not necessary for getting the world's work done. But differences, instead of being occasions for anxiety and exploitation, can be understood to be opportunities for harmony.

From a Christian point of view, the meaning of history is transformed once the Cross is essential. The difficulties of the world will not break us. There will be problems to be dealt with, and in dealing with them responsible people will be still under the obligation to do the best they can with what they have where they are, realizing that they are neither all-wise nor all-loving in making their plans and decisions. But in a vital way the faith of the Psalmist now rings true: "The Lord is King, be the people never so impatient; he sitteth between the Cherubim, be the earth never so unquiet."

The Christian Faith Beyond History

The Christian faith lived in history and the Christian faith transforming the meaning of history both point to God, the Father, as Lord not only of history but beyond history. In a wonderful meditation on Psalm 73, "Truly God is loving unto Israel, even to them of a clean heart," Martin Buber, the great Jewish thinker, says this: "It is as if the father took his little son's hand in the dark, not to do his walking for him, but to let him know through the warm pulsing of coursing blood that he, the father, was there."

Paul Tillich has made interesting use of a contrast between two Greek words, *chronos,* the time sequence, and *kairos,* the illuminating moment. By *chronos* he means the course of history understood and experienced as event after event, with cause and result, with action and reaction in the flow of life. The *kairos* moments are, however, the special gift of God— unpredictable, not to be contrived—which light up the meaning of the human situation, so that for the moment all the pieces seem to fall into place, and we know where we are, and somehow see over the horizon of time. We can grasp the distinction intellectually, but to feel it, to know it, to appreciate it—this is the gift itself. It is not possible for us to have more than inklings of what it means to refer to God as Lord of history and beyond history, but we do have inklings and these are significant.

People are always tempted to try to freeze their *kairos*

moments. In the Transfiguration story of the Synoptic Gospels, Peter proposed to build three tabernacles—one for Jesus, one for Moses, and one for Elijah—when he, James and John had their illuminating insight that Jesus was to be understood in an even greater light than Moses, the founder of the Jewish mission, and Elijah, the re-inspirer of straying Israel. Then the little group came down from the mountain to deal with the problem of the epileptic boy. For humans, the glimpse over the horizon of history is in order to be able to deal more effectively with the responsibilities of history.

St. Paul told the Romans: "What then shall we say to this? If God be for us, who is against us? He who did not spare his own Son but gave him up for us all, will he not also give us all things with him? . . . Who shall separate us from the love of Christ? Shall tribulation, or distress, or persecution, or famine, or nakedness, or peril, or sword? . . . No, in all these things we are more than conquerors through him who loved us. For I am sure that neither death, nor life, nor angels, nor principalities, nor things present, nor things to come, nor powers, nor height nor depth, nor anything else in all creation, will be able to separate us from the love of God in Christ Jesus our Lord." What St. Paul knew then, not only with his mind but even more profoundly in his heart, is still true, even in our modern era of cultural unsettlement.